Sparks of Redemptive Grace is not just another book for families dealing with mental illness; it is an experience for all of us. Merging the reality of pain with faith in Christ, Downing beautifully intertwines the two into a grieving interpretation of the heart, the Word of God and the prayers that find God weeping, rejoicing and answering us. Her pain seems to fuel our own eyes of faith as Downing takes us beyond mental illness to see "God shine His peace" into our secret places. This book is not about having the answers, but something far greater ... finding comfort and hope unshakable.

—**Joe Padilla**, CEO & Co-Founder,
Mental Health Grace Alliance

Catherine P. Downing has given Christian families a rare and long-awaited gift in *Sparks of Redemptive Grace: Seeking and Seeing God Amid a Loved One's Mental Illness.* As the mother of an adult child who suffers from clinical depression and chronic anxiety, her book provides a balm for my soul. She seamlessly weaves together intimate personal experiences, powerful prayers of the heart and scriptural promises to remind me, my family and my church that God's love is overwhelmingly unconditional, unceasing and always available for His imperfect children. With poignant wisdom, she underlines the truth that we are never alone in our sufferings, that no one is ever lost and that healing grace is abundant from a God who not only made us, but also suffers with us. *Sparks of Redemptive Grace* is an invaluable resource for all families of faith that can be used again and again as a prayerful devotion. It should be placed in every church library!

Valerie Holcombe,
NAMI Four Seasons "Bridges of Hope" promoter

This inspirational description of a Christian family's walk alongside a loved one with mental illness paints a realistic picture that is heartfelt yet simultaneously heart-breaking. *Sparks of Redemptive Grace* says much that other families experience every day but can never say out loud. The Downings' strength is that they never stray from their constant hope and faith.

—**Alice Zaccarello,** Executive Director,
The Well Community

Downing's marvelous account of her response to the reality of having a loved one with a serious mental health challenge is a must-read. If you have ever struggled to love a difficult person, especially one with a severe mental health condition, you will benefit from reading this book. It is deeply spiritual and deeply encouraging.

Written with marvelous honesty, modesty and candor, *Sparks of Redemptive Grace* illustrates how to build faith and trust in a most difficult circumstance. Downing has been given the opportunity to grow into mature faith in the face of (really, because of) unrelenting challenge. The heartbreak of a loved one's disability is poignantly addressed with beautiful prayers such as this: "O God, Who is love, teach me to love…reduce me to love." You, too, will be reduced to love as you read this book.

Barbara Ryan, mother of a severely handicapped
daughter, former lawyer and pastor's wife,
addiction and recovery lay counselor

Written with the compassion, vulnerability and yearning of a mother's heart, Downing offers poignant keyhole glimpses of her pilgrim journey with God and her son through the uncharted territory of his mental illness. If a picture paints a thousand words, Downing's powerful word pictures illustrate volumes. Caught up in her candid, grace-filled reflections, I twisted and turned with her in her wrestlings with denial and acceptance, despair and hope, brokenness and surrender. Describing the indescribable, *Sparks of Redemptive Grace* is a gift to anyone who can't find words to express the emotional chaos of living with someone suffering from mental illness, and points the way toward finding certainty in God in the midst of daily uncertainties. This book is also a gift for professionals, enabling them to vicariously experience the emotional and spiritual impact of mental illness on the family system. And, for friends, extended family members or pastors wanting to understand and support those who care for mentally ill loved ones, this profound book will change your perspective—maybe your life.

—**Carol Floch McColl**, M.A., LPC;
Author, *The Single Mom's Devotional* (2010, Baker.)

Though *Sparks of Redemptive Grace* is Downing's story, it is actually the story of millions who care for a mentally ill loved one—including me. Written from an intensely intimate and transparent perspective, Downing offers keen insight into the expectations and disappointments we experience daily. I thank her—we all thank her—for writing our story for us! In these few pages, Downing beautifully intertwines information with inspiration, and insight with encouragement, leaving the reader with a gut-wrenching hope and a hunger to know the God she does. Downing's prayers are poetry and her narration is captivating. It only takes an hour to read *Sparks of Redemptive Grace*, but don't rush it. Savor it. Meditate on it. Pray through it. And then share it with others.

Buzz Moody, Mental Health Grace Alliance Board Member and NAMI Dallas Family-to-Family trainer

SPARKS OF REDEMPTIVE GRACE

**Seeking and Seeing God
Amid a Loved One's
Mental Illness**

In your light do we see light.
—Psalm 36:9b (ESV)

SPARKS OF REDEMPTIVE GRACE

Seeking and Seeing God
Amid a Loved One's
Mental Illness

Catherine P. Downing

www.hispubg.com
A division of HISpecialists, llc

Printed in the United States of America
ISBN-13: 978-0-578-17717-5

First Edition: December 2015
10 9 8 7 6 5 4 3 2

CONTENTS

PREFACE

T he following story is only partly mine. It also belongs to others. I have been given the choice to share what I have lived, but they have not. And so, to respect their privacy, I have renamed us all and avoided any details that might disclose who we are. But we are real, and this is our reality.

ACKNOWLEDGMENTS

B ecause this book is written with pseudonyms to protect the privacy of our family, I am not able to list the full names of those who deserve grateful acknowledgment of their participation in bringing these words into print. Their full names and loving faces are etched forever in our hearts, but here they are listed by first name or initials only: JSD, DPD, Christa, Cathy, Julia Anne, Dianne, Gwynne, Beverly, Karen, Lynn and Bill.

In addition to those who helped with the manuscript, there is a very wide circle of friends and loved ones who walk this journey with us. They weep when we weep. They rejoice when we rejoice. And they pray always. We know who they are, and so does God. Our gratitude for their companionship is eternal.

If there are heroes in this story, they are the siblings. Their brother will never comprehend the incredible generosity they have expended on him, but may they know the vast expanse of their parents' grateful love.

INTRODUCTION

M y husband, Nelson, once said if we ever write a book the title should be, *It Wasn't Supposed to be Like This*. And surely the words are true. But I wonder if that phrase isn't actually already the subtitle for the Bible. After all, there are only two chapters at the beginning of the Scriptures and a few at the end that tell how things are "supposed to be." The rest of the Bible is about how things really are and about the unfolding story of God's redemptive grace to set things right again.

When Nelson and I started our life together, it was supposed be perfect. Our naive love would mature into true love. From our union would come children— healthy, smart and pretty. Although we hadn't a clue about parenting, we would learn in on-the-job training fashion. We would serve God as a family, with all our heart, soul and strength, going to the ends of the earth to declare His glory among the nations. That is how it was supposed to be. Now comes the rest of our book.

TEACHER OF LOVE

I will never forget one day in Venezuela when I went to visit a family who had given us a lamb. I went to thank them and there I found out that they had a badly crippled child. I asked the mother, "What is the child's name?" The mother gave me a most beautiful answer, "We call him 'Teacher of Love,' because he keeps on teaching us how to love. Everything we do for him is our love for God in action."
— Mother Teresa,
No Greater Love

After a few years of imperfect marriage, it seemed the right time to start our perfect family. While Nelson and I were both eager, we each were also terrified. Neither of us had had good role models for our respective father/mother jobs. I had unformed and unarticulated fears about passing on weaknesses from my family tree to my progeny. But we prayed about it and God answered.

It wasn't the first or last time God spoke to me clearly, but it turns out it was one of the most prophetic. Two truths burned through my fears. Like another mother, Mary, I have kept these things of God in my heart and have thought about them often. First, God reminded me that though I was ill-equipped and untrained to be a mother, I could be a good one, if I depended on Him. "Apart from Me you can do nothing," Jesus told His disciples. I knew this to be true. I had to abide in Him in order to be a good wife, friend, Sunday school teacher or neighbor. So, yes, to be a good mom, I would need to embed myself in the redemptive grace of God.

Secondly, and in the end, most profoundly, God assured me that He wouldn't give Nelson and me *a* child, but would give us *the* child — the one that He would specifically and deliberately design for us. At the time, I thought that meant we'd have a child who needed to learn love from us. I didn't understand that He was actually going to give us *the* child who would teach us to love.

REFLECTIVE PRAYER

For you formed my inward parts; you knitted me together in my mother's womb. I praise you, for I am fearfully and wonderfully made. Wonderful are your works; my soul knows it very well. My frame was not hidden from you, when I was being made in secret, intricately woven in the depths of the earth. Your eyes saw my unformed substance; in your book were written, every one of them, the days that were formed for me, when as yet there was none of them.

—Psalm 139:13-16 (ESV)

O Creator Father, at the moment of conception, Your skillful hands began to craft my son's body. At the very beginning You masterfully laid out the myriads of neurotransmitters in his brain, already knowing which ones would fail him. Before his lungs sucked in their first breath of life, You were aware of the smoke that would fill them. While You fashioned his feet, You saw the winding dark paths they would follow, and as You formed his arms, You knew the scars that would narrate his story.

And yet, O Lord, wonderful is all You make. Whatever You form, You declare it good. And so I praise You for creating him. I thank You that in the secret mysteries of Your plans You brought his life through my life. You knew the day when his pain would become my pain and my prayers would become his. Help me to trust that You "who began a good work will complete it." Amen.

CASE STUDY

A mental illness is a condition that impacts a person's thinking, feeling or mood and may affect his or her ability to relate to others and function on a daily basis. ...

1 in 5 adults experiences a mental health condition every year. One in 20 lives with a serious mental illness such as schizophrenia or bipolar disorder.

50% of mental health conditions begin by age 14 and 75% develop by age 24. The normal personality and behavior changes of adolescence may mimic or mask symptoms of a mental health condition.

—National Alliance for
Mental Illness

From the beginning, Douglas challenged our sensibilities. Normal infant colic, toddler defiance, and childhood impulsivity were all magnified exponentially in both intensity and duration. The first psychologist, after several rounds of tests, swiftly pronounced her inadequate diagnosis, while adding that she always recognized ADD children by the way their mothers collapsed into the chair in her office.

Nelson and I, exhausted and exasperated, had desperately recited the symptoms as though we had just discovered a unique and bizarre abnormality in humankind. But by the time we left her office, we had been corrected. Apparently our tale had already been written as a case study in a textbook for counselors. Though bizarre, the story of our son was not unique. There was no comfort in this fact—neither in knowing we weren't alone nor in knowing other families had to walk the same path.

The therapist to missionary families during Douglas' high school years overseas tried to ease our concerns as he matter-of-factly explained, "Many missionary kids find creative ways to 'act-out' while adjusting to a new culture. And of course, teenagers in any setting are prone to strong mood swings." Yes, this was our first teenager and our first cross-cultural adventure. But it wasn't our first inkling that we still hadn't found the right page in the textbook.

REFLECTIVE PRAYER

"Or imagine a woman who has ten coins and loses one. Won't she light a lamp and scour the house, looking in every nook and cranny until she finds it? And when she finds it you can be sure she'll call her friends and neighbors: 'Celebrate with me! I found my lost coin!' Count on it—that's the kind of party God's angels throw every time one lost soul turns to God."
—Luke 15:8-10 (The Message)

O Seeker of the lost and Savior of the sinner, find my son. Unlike the one sheep that wandered away from the flock or the prodigal who rebelled and ran to ruin, this son didn't lose his own way. Instead he silently and slowly just disappeared. O yes, he was evaluated, diagnosed and prescribed. He was scrutinized, analyzed and enrolled. But still no one could see him. And now, sucked into a vortex of delusion, he is lost even to me.

But You, O Light of the World, can shine Your love into the deepest corners and see the unseen. You can peek under the paperwork piled in the crannies and sweep out bureaucratic nooks. And You will. You will keep searching, always and forever, until You find Your treasure. So, I wait and I listen for Your celebration shout inviting me to the party Your angels will throw just for him. Amen.

CALDRON OF CHAOS

Bipolar disorder, also known as manic-depressive illness, is a brain disorder that causes unusual shifts in mood, energy, activity levels, and the ability to carry out day-to-day tasks. Symptoms of bipolar disorder are severe.

—National Institute of
Mental Health

Mania is the Greek word for madness. It is derived from mainmai, to rave in anger...

Mania is an abnormally elevated mood state characterized by such symptoms as inappropriate elation, increased irritability, severe insomnia, grandiose notions, increased speed and/or volume of speech, disconnected and racing thoughts, increased sexual desire, markedly increased energy and activity level, poor judgment, and inappropriate social behavior.

—MedicineNet.com

It was the psychiatrist called to the rural county jail back home who finally attached the right label. Afterwards, we each tried many times to peel it off. Nelson and I cowered uneasily under a tight cloak of denial. Yes, Douglas was a little "off," but our son would not become one of "them" — those people who walk up and down the streets talking to invisible friends, running from imaginary foes, those disheveled folks who smell bad and bother decent folks. Not our son. But after endless payments for bail, fines, property damages and attorney fees; numerous mental health warrants and repeat visits to psychiatric wards; and apologies ad nauseum to his girlfriends, our families and friends, we finally ripped off our denial and super-glued his label.

For Douglas, it was and is harder. The very part of our minds that helps us see and accept reality is the very part of his brain that is disconnected. And though there is an elusive and invisible line between *won't* and *can't*, it is clear that Douglas doesn't know how very sick he is.

This lack of awareness is a cruel master, forbidding him to seek treatment, blocking him from asking for help. So, for much of his life and for many of his days, Douglas lives in mania. He dances on the ledge and occasionally dives forcefully into the dark depths of madness.

REFLECTIVE PRAYER

In the beginning, God created the heavens and the earth. The earth was without form and void, and darkness was over the face of the deep. And the Spirit of God was hovering over the face of the waters.
—Genesis 1:1-2 (ESV)

O Creator Father, at the beginning of time, Your Spirit hovered over the swirling confusion. You spoke peace into the turmoil and brought order to that which was not yet made. Into the gurgling caldron of dark chaos, You poured quiet peace. Then You took that which was shapeless and formed it into firmness, solid and strong. And finally, as the climax of

Your goodness, within the incubator of Eden, You fashioned someone to love.

O Maker of all, at this time in my son's world, there is dark chaos. Confusion fills the emptiness, and a wind of wildness whips across the vast expanse of his soul. Break open his darkness with Your light. Form firm footing for his feet and steady his steps on solid ground. Fill his hollow spaces with Your love. Amen.

LANGUAGE OF LOSS

The realization that a family member's mental illness may never go away is a crucial identity turning point in the care-giving career because it forces to the surface of consciousness an array of emotions that previously may have been only dimly felt.

—David A. Karp,
The Burden of Sympathy:
How Families Cope with Mental Illness

If the moment of our epiphany were drawn as a cartoon, the bubble above our heads would not show a light bulb. It would be a lightening bolt. I am not sure which one of us first said it out loud: "This means we will never return to the mission field"; but once it was said we couldn't take it back. We were numb. Surely something was amiss. This was not the script we'd written. It wasn't even the one we thought we'd read. Even so, it was ours.

The native language of mental illness is loss. Those who live with it often lose their dreams, their self-esteem and even their identity. Those who live with them often do the same. But there are also differences. Douglas' own brain has betrayed him. Promising grand schemes, giant plans and great glory, it has instead robbed him of even the primal gifts of intimacy, productivity and freedom.

As caregivers, our losses carry their own realities. First, unlike for Douglas, there is no ambush here. We know what we're giving up. We abandon the "right" to do ministry on our terms, the privilege of clinging to our plans for retirement, the security of having a financial cushion. Second, there is no delusion here. We know our job now is to mitigate against damages, mop up messes and navigate the truly crazy and fully dysfunctional mental health system.

Mental health experts describe major disorders as "persistent and severe." I've often thought that those are apt adjectives to attach to the grief we each have experienced. For as the tally of relentless losses mount, so the sorrow grows, ever-present and deep. Paralyzed and mute, our trembling tears become our prayers of lament.

REFLECTIVE PRAYER

How long, O Lord? Will you forget me forever? How long will you hide your face from me? How long must I take counsel in my soul and have sorrow in my heart all the day?

—Psalm 13:1,2a (ESV)

O God of compassion, release us from the grip of sadness and free us from choking fear. Year after year, we watch the unrelenting waves of rage swell within him and beat down any hope of rest. We see the tide shift and the current drag him beneath the surface over and over and over.

He is drowning again and we are helpless again. We would have saved him long ago, but he is so very far away and we have so little strength. How long, O Man of Sorrows, will You wait to walk upon the waves and lift him out of his tumult? How long, O Prince of Peace, before You bring us rest from our turmoil? Come, Lord Jesus, come. Amen.

SPARKS OF REDEMPTIVE GRACE

Dearest Lord, may I see you today and everyday in the person of your sick, and while nursing them, minister to you. Though you hide yourself behind the unattractive disguise of the irritable, the exacting, the unreasonable, may I still recognize you and say, "Jesus, my patient, how sweet it is to serve you."

—Mother Teresa,
A Gift for God

When I was a kid and when my kids were children, we played with sparklers. We waited until all around us was night. Then we would ignite the slender stick and watch the wild display of tiny sprinkles of light. The sparks burned out as soon as "Ooh" left our lips. But, for a short second, we could see.

Along the dark journey with Douglas, God's redemptive grace has sparkled. Brilliant and brief, it is just enough to remind us that He is here. We have seen it when a friend a 1,000 miles away sent an email to say that she saw Douglas at a mall near her home—a reassurance that our missing son was safe. Or when a non-religious relative marveled at how steadfastly we've gripped our God over all this time and began to consider faith for himself. Or when a friend who struggles with depression observed how much better Douglas would be if he would just take medication, and then recognized the same could be true for her.

In these tiny bursts of light, we see glimpses of God at work. The work of God is to take the broken, the lost, the hopeless and reflect from them His own redemptive grace and goodness. Nowhere have Nelson and I seen this more clearly than in our own hearts.

In loving Douglas we have learned what it means to love. Loving him has taught us that love must be selfless, generous and forbearing. It must be patient and kind. And most of all, it must be from God. Even as parents, we can't

begin to come up with the kind of unconditional, unrelenting love that is required. But in
our darkest times, God's redemptive love
sparkles through us and we see grace.

REFLECTIVE PRAYER
Love never gives up.
Love cares more for others than for self.
Love doesn't want what it doesn't have.
Love doesn't strut,
Doesn't have a swelled head,
Doesn't force itself on others,
Isn't always "me first,"
Doesn't fly off the handle,
Doesn't keep score of the sins of others,
Doesn't revel when others grovel,
Takes pleasure in the flowering of truth,
Puts up with anything,
Trusts God always,
Always looks for the best,
Never looks back,
But keeps going to the end.
—I Corinthians 13:4-7 (The Message)

O God who is love, teach me to love. My
own love is so anemic and fleeting, and his

need for love is so cavernous and constant. Only Your love, infinite and fierce, is big enough for this. Blast the light of Your conquering love into my life. Purge out my lust for self-pity and gluttony for approval. Root out resentment. Unearth bitterness. Cleanse me from the deceptions of hypocrisy. Jesus, reduce me to love. Amen.

WHO ARE YOU?

"Who are you?" said the Caterpillar. This was not an encouraging opening for a conversation. Alice replied, rather shyly, "I–I hardly know, Sir, just at present–at least I knew who I was when I got up this morning, but I think I must have been changed several times since then."

— Lewis Carroll,
Alice's Adventures in Wonderland

In truth, there are two Douglases. There is the "not-well" Douglas and the "well-er" Douglas. When he is in a manic episode (sometimes lasting half the year), he is very not-well. He does not sleep, does not stop talking, does not sit still, does not let you talk, does not let you sleep. He's agitated and irritable. His big — very big — ideas need lots of wall space on which they can be detailed. Codes of words, numbers, and symbols stretch down his hall-way, written with the care of a St. John on Pat-mos, faithfully recording his revelations.

"Not-well" Douglas is always angry, and his dad is always to blame. He yells with rec-ognizable words put together in unintelligible sentences. The lexicon is small, so he uses pro-fanities to substitute for missing vocabulary. It's as though he's an adult stuck in a 2-year-old's tantrum day after day. It's hell for us as we listen. I can't even begin to imagine what it's like for him. What's worse than hell? It must be like that.

"Well-er" Douglas asks me how my day was. He tidies his room and mows my lawn. The same lips that last week shouted fervent vulgarities when he was asked to clear the ta-ble now whisper a quiet, sincere prayer when asked to say the dinner blessing. He gently thanks his dad for driving him to the store and tells us both that he loves us as he heads off to bed to sleep for 10 to 14 hours. Nelson and I retreat to our room to offer a prayer of guarded thanksgiving to Our-Father-Who-art-in-heaven. We are grateful for us all to be out of hell for a while.

REFLECTIVE PRAYER

O Lord, you have searched me and known me!
Where shall I go from your Spirit?
Or where shall I flee from your presence?
If I ascend to heaven, you are there!
If I make my bed in Sheol, you are there!
If I take the wings of the morning
and dwell in the uttermost parts of the sea,
even there your hand shall lead me,
and your right hand shall hold me.
If I say, "Surely the darkness shall cover me
and the light about me be night,"
even the darkness is not dark to you;
the night is bright as the day,
for darkness is as light with you.
—Psalm 139:1, 7-12 (ESV)

O all-knowing Lord, even when Douglas doesn't know who he is, You do. Even when I can't recognize this wild-eyed man as the infant who once gurgled at my breast and cooed to my lullabies, You know him. At other times, when sleep and mercy create an oasis of sanity, You recognize him. Thank You that he is never, never, never unknown.

O ever-present God, You who wait for Douglas in his high and lofty hopes and hold him through his deep and dark fears, thank You for never "leaving nor forsaking" him. Thank You that wherever his mind takes him, You will have already arrived. Whether in the hellish madness of mania or in the quieted stillness of a weary one at rest, You are there. Thank You that he is never, never, never alone.

O Father, who dwells in unapproachable light, O Christ, who is the light that has come into the world, O Spirit for whom the darkness is not dark, thank You for shining Your peace into Douglas' secret places. Thank You that even when he crawls into his imaginary camouflaged cave, You see him. Thank You that he is never, never, never hidden. Amen.

SECOND-HAND PAIN

Invisible *is the word normal children most often use to describe their place in the family. Their everyday trials and tribulations pale beside the catastrophe of their siblings' predicaments, so it seems natural that they should never come first. The chronic overlooking is rarely intentional. Rather, it is what happens when desperate, overwhelmed adults with problems of their own try to cope with situations that no parent bargains for and few have the emotional resources to balance. As a result, many healthy siblings grow up with a hunger for attention that is never satisfied and that seems wrong to feel.*

—Jeanne Safer,
The Normal One:
Life with a Difficult or Damaged Sibling

"Maybe not being here is his gift to us." One of the children bravely put words to the guilty delight we were all feeling, but not daring to admit. It was Christmas morning and Douglas was in the psychiatric hospital. How many family occasions has Douglas, in the throes of wild mania, ruined for his siblings? Enough. It has not just been events or holidays, though. Even in the routine days of life, he is able to suck all the attention directly to himself. He is the center. Always.

Nelson and I have talked often and sighed deeply over the profound toll Douglas' mental illness has exacted from the lives of our other children. Like victims of second-hand smoke, all have suffered. As they were growing up we tried hard to keep up with everyone's ball-games, piano lessons, church groups and homework. But we were less able to pay attention to their disappointments when the games were lost, to their embarrassments when they misplayed notes at the recitals or to their feelings of rejection by cliques in the youth groups. Our other children were never invisible to us, but at the same time, because our eyes were always watchful over Douglas, his siblings were never quite in focus.

In becoming adults each has had to find their own paths through the emotional carnage that was left in their hearts in the wake of a mentally ill oldest brother. Jonathan was born with an unusual capacity for relationship and intimacy. Like a twin in search of his other twin, from his earliest days he looked to Douglas to be his companion, confidant and champion. But Douglas would have none of it. He pushed Jonathan away time after time after time, enlarging the chasm of longing in Jonathan's sensitive heart. As an adult Jonathan now works hard to build healthy emotional bridges with others as he continues to wish for the brother who *should-have-been*.

Joanna watches Douglas with a bit of somber suspicion, wondering in what ways she is like him and how she can learn from what he doesn't know. She is frightened by the nascent notion that her brother's eyes might actually be mirrors. At the same time, Joanna is a willing companion for Douglas when he wants to hang out in the middle of the night at a greasy restaurant. Her empathy and kindness overcome the humiliating embarrassment that beckons her to run. Joanna adores Douglas with a humble and hopeful heart that embraces the brother who *could-yet-be*.

Douglas' siblings are strong, loving, gifted and grace-filled people. They were shaped like clay by God's skilled and tender hands, despite the fact that our family unit served as a very wobbly potter's wheel.

Reflective Prayer

"Then the King will say to those on his right, 'Come, you who are blessed by my Father, inherit the kingdom prepared for you from the foundation of the world. For I was hungry and you gave me food, I was thirsty and you gave me drink, I was a stranger and you welcomed me, I was naked and you clothed me, I was sick and you visited me, I was in prison and you

came to me.' Then the righteous will an-
swer him, saying, 'Lord, when did we see
you hungry and feed you, or thirsty and
give you drink? And when did we see you
a stranger and welcome you, or naked and
clothe you? And when did we see you sick
or in prison and visit you?' And the King
will answer them, 'Truly, I say to you, as
you did it to one of the least of these my
brothers, you did it to me.'"

—Matthew 25:34-40 (ESV)

O God, our perfect heavenly Father, who
fills the orphan with daily bread, feed the hungry places in our children's hearts. Be to them
what we, in our finiteness and fragility, could
not be. Lift their heads to see Your ever-atten-
tive face smiling with delight. Open their ears
to hear Your songs of joy breaking into their
ever-seeking souls.

O Jesus, our perfect elder brother, who has
invited us to come into the Father's kingdom,
take note of these our children who have car-
ried their brother to Your party. They have fed

him with love, quenched his thirst with their laughter and included him in their prayers.

O First-born among all, notice how these siblings have turned their cheeks so often they are whiplashed. They have given away so many shirts they are nearly stripped bare. Restore to them all they have lost, return all that has been taken, and redeem all they have given up. As they increasingly assume primary care for the one You also call brother, may they not be absorbed by his illness, nor weakened by his pain. Instead, may they see You in his face, and hear You say, "You did this to me. Well done." Amen.

DELIVER US

Demons are involved at many levels of our existence, and it certainly isn't necessary for demonic powers to purposefully cause a given mental illness in a person for us to be able to say that they were involved in the disorder. … All mental disorders result from the interaction of biology and environmental factors. We have a biology that is broken because of sin, and we live in an environment infected by the evil one. From this perspective the demonic is involved in all illness, including mental illness, at some level; and that reality may be why the Gospel authors so blurred the lines between "natural" illness and demonic infirmity.

—Matthew S. Stanford,
Grace for the Afflicted:
A Clinical and Biblical Perspective
on Mental Illness

When we first began this journey, I asked God for understanding so that I could pray effectively. How much of Douglas' troubles are brought on by his physical brain disorder? What about his own will and choices? How did specific traumatic events in his life damage him emotionally? How much influence does the demonic have in his struggles? Though God has graciously provided increasing understanding in all four arenas over the years, the response He gave early on is still the same truth I come back to over and over: "It doesn't so much matter the cause. I am the answer to all those aspects. Just keep bringing him to Me." Because He is the answer, I do.

However, at various times I have focused prayer specifically around one of the four arenas (physical, volitional, emotional, spiritual). For example, there are times when Douglas' behavior is so bizarre and destructive that the presence of evil is unmistakable. It is as though his tormentors have invaded the sacredness of his soul and set up shop. "Deliver from evil," then becomes the rallying call-to-arms. With fasting and the fortification of praying friends, we figuratively encircle Douglas, trusting Christ for his deliverance, watching for the release.

Sometimes the answer is displayed through the quieting of his mind just long enough to get a stretch of hard, long sleep. Other times we are emboldened to take heroic action to get him to medical help. And there are rare times when suddenly clarity prevails and he is able to listen to reason. But, each and every time we see the mighty authority of God setting this captive free, even if it's just long enough to remind us Whose is the kingdom, and the power and the glory.

REFLECTIVE PRAYER

They came to the other side of the sea, to the country of the Gerasenes. And when Jesus had stepped out of the boat, immediately there met him out of the tombs a man with an unclean spirit. He lived among the tombs. And no one could bind him anymore, not even with a chain, for he had often been bound with shackles and chains, but he wrenched the chains apart, and he broke the shackles in pieces. No one had the strength to subdue him. Night and day among the tombs and on the mountains he was always crying out and cutting himself with stones. ...

As he [Jesus] was getting into the boat, the man who had been possessed with demons begged him that he might be with him. And he did not permit him but said to him, "Go home to your friends and tell them how much the Lord has done for you, and how he has had mercy on you." And he went away and began to proclaim in the Decapolis how much Jesus had done for him, and everyone marveled.

—Mark 5:1-5; 18-20 (ESV)

Feared, yet afraid. Empowered, yet impotent. Outcast and alone. Homeless and helpless. That is how the man was, until You came.

Jesus, You arrived after sailing through a storm so terrific and terrible Your disciples assumed there was no hope of survival. But You delivered all to safety. For You have the authority to calm waves and quiet winds.

And when You landed in the country of the Gerasenes, You did the one thing You came to do. You delivered a tormented soul from his demons. For You have the authority to cast out evil and heal the afflicted.

After You sent him back to his family, restoring him to his community, You got back in Your boat and left.

O Jesus, would You now set Your sail for our shore? Amen.

BEAUTIFUL

Will you be my friend?
A friend
Who far beyond the feebleness
of any vow or tie
Will touch the secret place
where I am really I,
To know the pain of lips that plead
and eyes that weep,
Who will not run away
when you find me in the street
Alone and lying mangled
by my quota of defeats
But will stop and stay—
to tell me of another day
When I was beautiful.
—James Kavanaugh,
Will you be my Friend?

I am the de facto contact for Lynnette, a precious friend who has breast cancer. I send notices to keep friends aware of how well the drugs are valiantly fighting against this horrid intruder and how bravely our sweet friend stands strong on the faith of others. We all know that the cancer is uninvited and unwelcome. Any time I inform people of her illness I always say, "Lynnette has cancer." Never once have I said, "Lynnette is cancer."

While mining in the old medical files Douglas released to me, I unearthed this note from one of his psychologists: "Patient reports tension with his family. He believes his parents only see him as his illness and not as himself." It is a heartbreaking truth that I had to learn to think and to say, "Douglas has bipolar disorder," instead of, "Douglas is bipolar." A minor wording difference. A monumental identity distinction. To have a disease, rather than to be one, is a defining stance of dignity.

Douglas is not his illness. He is a beloved child of God, and of ours. He is a young man with gifts, talents and dreams. He is clever, handsome and generous. But when his brain flips into its manic mode, all those truths about who he really is seem to go into hibernation, and all we see is crazy.

The fact is, we are all flawed, in myriad ways. And not one of us wants to be defined by those broken parts or weaknesses. So we work hard to hide our frailties and mask our fallenness. With Douglas, his fractured brain has stripped him of the ability to cover up what he—and we—would much rather hide. So he aggressively rants on, psychologically naked and emotionally exposed. Raw and revealed.

Lynnette is also not at her best these days. Her hair is gone. Her clothes drip from her too-thin shoulders. Her eyes are sad and scared. But when we see her, we don't see her illness, we see her. She is not cancer. She is Lynnette. And she is beautiful.

Reflective Prayer

Now when Jesus came into the district of Caesarea Philippi, he asked his disciples, "Who do people say that the Son of Man is?" And they said, "Some say John the Baptist, others say Elijah, and others Jeremiah or one of the prophets." He said to them, "But who do you say that I am?" Simon Peter replied, "You are the Christ, the Son of the living God." And Jesus answered him, "Blessed are you, Simon Bar-Jonah! For flesh and blood has not revealed this to you, but my Father who is in heaven. And I tell you, you are Peter, and on this rock I will build my church, and the gates of hell shall not prevail against it."

—Matthew 16:13-18 (ESV)

O Messiah, Son of the living God, even You longed to be known rightly. When others saw You as who You were not, You sought out those who could recognize who You are.

When Peter declared Your identity, You, in turn, declared his. Even though he would later flail and flounder in the bog of denial, You saw,

You knew and You proclaimed him to be strong and steady. Even though You regularly had to sequester his impulsivity, You anchored him as the foundational rock of Your yet-to-be Church.

O all-seeing God, who looks upon Douglas through the lens of eternal love and declares him precious in Your sight, heal our blurry vision. Enable us to look past his all-too-obvious illness and clearly see Your beautiful beloved covered in Your regal robe of grace. Amen

FEAR FIGHT

From childhood's hour I have not been
As others were—I have not seen
As others saw—I could not bring
My passions from a common spring—
From the same source I have not taken
My sorrow—I could not awaken
My heart to joy at the same tone—
And all I lov'd—I lov'd alone—

—Edgar Allan Poe,
Alone

Then there are the silent days when the bipolar pendulum swings to depression. For Douglas, this is rare. For us, it is just as frightening as the manic phase.

Every 12.3 minutes[1] depression takes another life in the United States. Though depression is the dormant mode of bipolar disorder order for Douglas, it is the dominant one for

---

[1] Center for Disease Control and Prevention

most people with this illness. Joining Major Depressive Disorder and other factors, bipolar depression contributed to suicide's ranking in the list of top 10 killers in the U.S. In fact, according to the American Foundation for Suicide Prevention, "90% of those who die by suicide had a diagnosable psychiatric disorder at the time of their death."

During Douglas's depression cycle, hyper-vigilance regularly awakens Nelson and me from our sleep to make sure he has not been consumed by the night. In the day, we sit with him in his solitude, trusting that our presence mystically reassures him that he isn't alone, that he's loved. And we desperately pray-to-God that that is enough.

Whether Douglas is sinking in depression or soaring in mania, I am always slogging through fear. Again and again, as I fight the fright, Jesus takes my chubby cheeks firmly in His hands, and like a mother with a terrified toddler, redirects my eyes to His. He holds me in His arms of reassuring love and redemptive grace. Nestled there, I find peace and with it the confidence to boldly hope the same for Douglas.

REFLECTIVE PRAYER

"Peace I leave with you; my peace I give to you. Not as the world gives do I give to you. Let not your hearts be troubled, neither let them be afraid."

—John 14:27 (ESV)

Generous Jesus, help Douglas and me to accept the gift of peace that is ours for the taking. Help us not put it on the shelf or toss it in the closet as we do with other gifts. Instead, may we unwrap Your gift of peace with gratitude and wrap ourselves in it with thanksgiving.

Gracious Lord, though our broken hearts all too easily let fear take charge, give us power to not let that happen. Cast out these fears with Your perfect love. Be the glory and lifter of our heads so we may behold Your goodness in the land of the living. Amen.

SINS AND ENCUMBRANCES

*The soul is not the seat of sickness in the
mentally ill; it is the brain, its synapses
and receptors and so on, that render the
mind broken. The soul, as the self in rela-
tion to God, continues healthy in anyone
as long as that person is in Christ, relating to and witnessing to God.*

—Kathryn Greene-McCreight,
*Darkness Is My Only Companion:
A Christian Response to Mental Illness*

We were sitting in the guidance counselor's office in the mission high school overseas. She
had just delivered the bad news about Douglas'
grades and the possibility that he might not
graduate with his class. Now, at that point, all
we knew was that though very intelligent,
Douglas was dealing with ADD and some
learning disabilities. We were not yet aware
we were gradually approaching the precipice
of a mental illness.

After the counselor left the room, I turned to Douglas and admonished him from Hebrews, stating that he must "lay aside every sin and encumbrance" that was tripping him up. I explained that only he was able to know whether his poor grades were because of learning challenges (encumbrances) or because of laziness (sin). In the end, we didn't sort that out, but somehow he did miraculously get through school. As I told the guidance counselor while showing her his diploma on his scheduled graduation day, "Indeed, there is a God. And He does answer prayer!"

I am still confident there is a God, but I am never quite sure how He and Douglas relate to each other. Over the last sixteen years, as the encumbrances have become more debilitating and sins more detrimental, I have continued to struggle with questions of culpability and responsibility. How does God judge the sinful deeds committed in the throes of a mind gone manic? How does He manifest the power of

His redemptive grace while tending the encumbrances of Douglas' soul? How does
Douglas hear God call his name amid the
clamor of all the other voices in his head? How
does the Holy Spirit show him right from
wrong, good from bad, sacred from profane,
lazy from distracted? Where, in all the confusion of his mind, does Douglas find Jesus?
How does he experience the love, forgiveness
and kindness of the Savior who died for his
sins? What does the risen Christ and the power
of His resurrection look like in Douglas' life?

REFLECTIVE PRAYER

*But Mary stood weeping outside the tomb,
and as she wept she stooped to look into
the tomb. And she saw two angels in
white, sitting where the body of Jesus had
lain, one at the head and one at the feet.
They said to her, "Woman, why are you
weeping?" She said to them, "They have
taken away my Lord, and I do not know
where they have laid him." Having said
this, she turned around and saw Jesus*

> *standing, but she did not know that it was Jesus. Jesus said to her, "Woman, why are you weeping? Whom are you seeking?" Supposing him to be the gardener, she said to him, "Sir, if you have carried him away, tell me where you have laid him, and I will take him away." Jesus said to her, "Mary." She turned and said to him in Aramaic, "Rabboni!" (which means Teacher).*

—John 20:11-16 (ESV)

O Risen Lord, when Douglas looks for You, are You hidden? Like the sun that is covered by drifting clouds, do You seem to come and go? There in the sanity, gone in the madness? Are You, the One that he loved yesterday, taken away today, leaving him confused and scared? Send Your ministering angels, Lord, to tell him where You are, to show him the way to find You again.

O Teacher, help him to learn the sound of Your voice as You call him by name. Show him how to recognize You when You appear in unexpected places, looking to him more like the gardener than his Lord. Stir up in him the desire to find You, even if he has to "go and get" You.

O Mighty God, reveal to him the grace of the cross that forgives sin and the power of the resurrection that conquers encumbrances. Then teach him the difference between the two, so he might confess the one, and overcome the other, laying aside both at the throne of Your empty tomb. Amen.

CASSEROLES

*I believe Christ is calling his church to a
great outpouring of love, overflowing
from the bottomless well of living water
he has placed within each of his people. I
believe he wants that love to reach people
with mental illness and lift them in a
great wave of healing and hope—right
where they are, among those our society
considers untouchable, avoidable and jus-
tifiably condemned to the fringes.*

—Amy Simpson,
Troubled Minds:
Mental Illness and the Church's Mission

It is sometimes called the "no casserole" illness,
because when a loved one has a severe bout
with a mental illness, no one from the church
brings over a meal, like they do for gall blad-
der surgery, cancer treatments or even child-
birth. The fact of the matter is, though a pastor
is often the first person turned to when a men-

tal illness begins to surface, the church is typically the last responder to this kind of family crisis. Why is that?

There are lots of reasons, including fear, ignorance, confusion and anemic or distorted doctrines related to suffering in general and mental illness in particular. Often though, the family itself doesn't let its suffering be known. Family members' own fear, ignorance and confusion block the openness needed to receive the "outpouring of love" Christ desires to stream through His church.

In desperate need for emotional and spiritual support, Nelson and I risked transparency. In response, with hesitant and stumbling baby steps, our church has started growing into a conduit of strength and comfort. Casseroles from people in our church come from a variety of menus. They serve up generous portions of fervent prayers, kind words, attentive phone calls and multiple offers of help. Most nourishing of all are those that come with listening ears and shared tears.

Because of the nature of mental illness, it is likely that our needs will not go away. There will be many Sundays when we melt before the altar in a puddle of hopeless despair. Douglas' name will stay a permanent entry on the prayer list. The church is learning that to love us well, they must love us long. Over time, we will need many, many more casseroles.

REFLECTIVE PRAYER

The way God designed our bodies is a model for understanding our lives together as a church: every part dependent on every other part, the parts we mention and the parts we don't, the parts we see and the parts we don't. If one part hurts, every other part is involved in the hurt, and in the healing. If one part flourishes, every other part enters into the exuberance.

—1 Corinthians 12:25-26 (The Message)

O ever-wise God, is it possible that our church needs Douglas as much as we need them? Could it be that You have put us in this body at this time so they could be a part of the comfort You are pouring out upon our family? Are we, perhaps, merely mirrors for others to see their own camouflaged hurts? Are we heralds inviting others to uncloak their neediness and to come to You for hope and healing?

O all-seeing Lord, show Your Church those who suffer among us, hidden away beneath blankets of stigma, shoved into corners of marginalization. You who call Your Body to care for the least, the lost, the lonely, the left-behind, teach us how to include those whom others deem unworthy. Bless us with the opportunity to become a community where they can flourish. Amen.

FEEBLE FAITH

*We should be astonished at the goodness
of God, stunned that He should bother to
call us by name, our mouths wide open at
His love, bewildered that at this very mo-
ment we are standing on holy ground.*
— Brennan Manning,
The Ragamuffin Gospel:
Good News for the Bedraggled,
Beat-Up, and Burnt Out

We pray a lot for Douglas. We pray with others, we pray individually, we pray silently, we
pray with words, we pray with tears, we pray
at our church's altar, we pray in the car and we
pray beside Douglas' bed as he sleeps. Like the
four friends who lowered their loved one
through a hole in the roof, we carry Douglas to
Jesus any way we can.

Recently, during a particularly prolonged
and destructive manic episode, we tried three

times to get Douglas to medical help. Each attempt was thwarted. As we cried, prayed and fasted, the idea came to ask 30 friends from coast to coast to set aside two hours on a particular evening to enter a focused time of intercession. Ten local folks gathered in our home. Others joined in spirit from afar.

About two weeks later, the manic episode ended abruptly. Within a month Douglas agreed to go on medication (for the first time in years), to participate in an outpatient treatment program and to start seeing a therapist. But most profoundly, he began to see how this illness, untreated, destroys so much of who he is, what he loves and those who care for him.

Looking through the rubble left from the manic craziness, Douglas was sobered by the scope and depth of the damage. In the language of recovery, Douglas "hit bottom." This jolted him to his senses so powerfully that he miraculously acknowledged his illness and welcomed medical help. After a dozen years of denials, this breakthrough was stunning.

I was thrilled. I was relieved. I was thankful. But, to be honest, mostly I was shocked.

And then I was ashamed. My reaction had exposed an unsettling reality of faith. How could I believe enough to call a group together to pray, only to be amazed when God responded as they had asked? How could I pray so often, so passionately, so carefully myself, only to be so utterly astonished by this answer? Could it be that I am deceived to think my prayers reveal great faith, when actually they aren't much more than compulsive wishful thinking?

Or could the truer insight be that all faith is a mustard seed, all belief is coupled with unbelief and when we confidently step out onto the water it is always just long enough to need to be rescued. Perhaps within each of us who boldly confronts a giant Goliath, there pounds the heart of a doubting Thomas. For in the end, perhaps God's greatest delight is to remind us that it's less about our faith and more about His redemptive grace. For no matter how strong or small our expectations, no matter how fervent or feeble our faith, it is He who "is able to do far more abundantly than all that we ask or think." (Ephesians 3:20 ESV)

REFLECTIVE PRAYER

So Peter was kept in prison, but earnest prayer for him was made to God by the church.

Now when Herod was about to bring him out, on that very night, Peter was sleeping between two soldiers, bound with two chains, and sentries before the door were guarding the prison. And behold, an angel of the Lord stood next to him, and a light shone in the cell. He struck Peter on the side and woke him, saying, "Get up quickly." And the chains fell off his hands. And the angel said to him, "Dress yourself and put on your sandals." And he did so. And he said to him, "Wrap your cloak around you and follow me." And he went out and followed him. He did not know that what was being done by the angel was real, but thought he was seeing a vision. When they had passed the first and

*the second guard, they came to the iron
gate leading into the city. It opened for
them of its own accord, and they went out
and went along one street, and immediately the angel left him. When Peter came
to himself, he said, "Now I am sure that
the Lord has sent his angel and rescued
me from the hand of Herod and from all
that the Jewish people were expecting."*

*When he realized this, he went to the
house of Mary, the mother of John whose
other name was Mark, where many were
gathered together and were praying. And
when he knocked at the door of the gate-
way, a servant girl named Rhoda came to
answer. Recognizing Peter's voice, in her
joy she did not open the gate but ran in
and reported that Peter was standing at
the gate. They said to her, "You are out of
your mind." But she kept insisting that it
was so, and they kept saying, "It is his
angel!" But Peter continued knocking,
and when they opened, they saw him and
were amazed.*

—Acts 12:5-16 (ESV)

O Faithful One, who with power and compassion sets captives free, fill my faithless heart so full of trust that I am never surprised by Your answers, only overwhelmed by Your goodness. Help me to know You so well that I believe steadfastly when You are quiet in Your love with the same confidence I have when Your might is gloriously displayed.

O Glad God, may I come to know You as the one who loves to lavish favor upon Your children and is always ready to respond to their prayers with the very best answer dispensed at the very right time. When You swing open doors of my captivity, may I follow You out. When You knock at the door of my heart, may I welcome You in. When I see Your presence where I never expected You to be, may I not be embarrassed with astonishment but dazzled with joy. Amen.

EVER AFTER

Each day he comes home with
a new bag of magic beans.
O Lord, give him good soil
where he can plant his dreams.
　　　　　　—Poem I wrote for Douglas
　　　　　　　　when he was four

When a child dies at an early age, a mother's dreams for that little one become nightmares. The "what-ifs" torment. The "could-have-beens" prick the heart. Who would my child have become? What great things might they have done? Would she have solved world hunger? Would he have cured leukemia?

Like other mothers whose dreams for their children's lives are taken through death, prolonged dying or severely incapacitated living, I often wonder what my son would be accomplishing if mental illness had not hijacked and commandeered his life. I see the full and successful lives his siblings enjoy and imagine

Douglas as a giver, not a taker, as a leader, not a disrupter. Maybe even as the curer of leukemia.

Often those with a profound mental illness get "stuck" at the level of emotional maturity and life stage they were in when the illness first struck. As the oldest, Douglas has watched his younger siblings move on through life phases of college and careers. Meanwhile he is marooned in adolescence, living in a chronic state of rebellious dependence.

In the depths of our beings, we feel the unfairness. The pain oozing from our fallen world often smears the vision of eternity that God has placed in our hearts. We live with the sorrow of "paradise lost" and the aching conviction that "this isn't how it is supposed to be." To survive, we fix our hopes in the place where leukemia and bipolar disorder are already cured. In heaven we will each be who God created and desires us to be, untainted by sin and unencumbered by the muck of this life.

Heaven is where the heaviness of disappointment is finally lifted and where the *could-bes* reach their full and unfettered potential. It will be there, someday, when I will meet Douglas again for the very first time.

REFLECTIVE PRAYER

Then I saw a new heaven and a new earth, for the first heaven and the first earth had passed away, and the sea was no more. And I saw the holy city, new Jerusalem, coming down out of heaven from God, prepared as a bride adorned for her husband.

And I heard a loud voice from the throne saying, "Behold, the dwelling place of God is with man. He will dwell with them, and they will be his people, and God himself will be with them as their God. He will wipe away every tear from their eyes, and death shall be no more, neither shall there be mourning, nor crying, nor pain anymore, for the former things have passed away."

> *And he who was seated on the throne said,*
> *"Behold, I am making all things new."*
> *Also he said, "Write this down, for these*
> *words are trustworthy and true."*
> —Revelation 21:1-5 (ESV)

O God, in Eden You placed eternity in our hands, and we dragged it through the dung of rebellion. So You removed the experience of it from our grasp and planted a hope for it in our hearts. You hid it somewhere safe and unsoiled and then You promised that someday, once we were clean, we could have it back.

O Jesus, through Your blood, You are removing our stains and restoring our health, so we can begin again, new and right. How gently You are readying Your bride, preparing us for the home You prepared for us.

O Holy Spirit, comfort us while we wait—fallen, frail, finite and fearful. Fill us with anticipation of better. Keep forever and ever after in plain sight that we may not lose heart or hope. You, who sealed us with the promise of everlasting life, preserve us until we return to the beginning and start over just the way it was supposed to be. Amen.

RESOURCES

All happy families are alike; each un-happy family is unhappy in its own way.
—Leo Tolstoy,
Anna Karenina

There is a cliff I walk along while trying to stay well away from the edge, and in writing these pages I have been very aware of its nearness. I have tried to stay on the narrow path between detached realism and narcissistic drama, for I know well that self-pity is a dangerous precipice and those who fall in often do not come back up.

So in relating our story, I have never once lost sight of others who have equal or harder stories of suffering. Many, many families tend to loved ones who are chronically ill, horribly debilitated and/or fully dependent on caregivers. The range of diseases is vast, and the toll on families enormous. And even within the ranks of those who care for the mentally ill (13.6 million[2] in the U.S. as a conservative estimate) our family's experience is neither unique nor even extreme.

It has been greatly helpful to Nelson and me — and to a lesser extent Douglas' siblings — to connect with and learn from other families who travel the same road. Two organizations have given tremendous support to us: Mental Health Grace Alliance (Christian) and the National Alliance on Mental Illness. They both offer well-researched resources, education programs and support groups. We have also been aided by a raft of other resources, both in print and online. I've listed a few in the next chapter.

[2] https://www.nami.org/Learn-More/Mental-Health-By-the-Numbers

BOOKS

Amador, Xavier. *I Am Not Sick I Don't Need Help: How to Help Someone with Mental Illness Accept Treatment.* New York: Vida Press. 2010.

Hinckley, Jack and Jo Ann Hinckley. *Breaking Points.* Grand Rapids, Michigan: Zondervan. 1985.

Karp, David A. *The Burden of Sympathy: How Families Cope with Mental Illness.* New York, New York: Oxford University Press. 2001.

Miklowitz, David J. *The Bipolar Disorder Survival Guide: What You and Your Family Need to Know.* New York, New York: Guilford Press. 2002.

Papolos, Demitri F. and Janice Papolos. *The Bipolar Child: The Definitive and Reassuring*

Guide to Childhood's Most Misunderstood Disorder. New York, New York: Broadway Books. 1999.

Simpson, Amy. *Troubled Minds: Mental Illness and the Church's Mission.* Downers Grove, IL: InterVarsity Press. 2013.

Stanford Matthew S. *Grace for the Afflicted: A Clinical and Biblical Perspective on Mental Illness.* Colorado Springs, CO: Paternoster Publishing. 2008.

ORGANIZATIONS
& ONLINE SOURCES

American Foundation for Suicide Prevention
https://www.afsp.org/

Bring Change 2 Mind
http://bringchange2mind.org/

International Bipolar Foundation
http://ibpf.org/

Mental Health and the Church
https://www.youtube.com/chan-
nel/UCIDSO5LF3RteManoNsTXzqQ

Mental Health Grace Alliance
http://mentalhealthgracealliance.org/

NAMI (National Alliance on Mental Illness)
https://www.nami.org

CREDITS BY CHAPTER

Teacher of Love

Teresa, Mother. *No Greater Love.* New York, New York: MJF Books, 1997.

Case Study

www.nami.org/Learn-More/Mental-Health-Conditions

Caldron of Chaos

"What Is Bipolar Disorder?" *National Institute of Mental Health,* accessed http://www.nimh.nih.gov/health/topics/bipo-lar-disorder/index.shtml

http://www.medicinenet.com

Language of Loss

Karp, David A. *The Burden of Sympathy: How Families Cope with Mental Illness.* New York, New York: Oxford University Press. 2001.

Sparkles of Redemptive Grace

Teresa, Mother. *A Gift for God.* New York, New York: Harper & Row. 1975.

Who are You?

Carroll, Lewis. *The Annotated Alice: Alice's Adventures in Wonderland and Through the Looking Glass.* New York, New York: Bramhall House. 1960.

Second-hand Pain

Safer, Jeanne. *The Normal One: Life with a Difficult or Damaged Sibling.* New York, New York: The Free Press. 2002.

Deliver Us

Stanford, Matthew S. *Grace for the Afflicted: A Clinical and Biblical Perspective on Mental Illness.* Colorado Springs, CO: Paternoster Publishing. 2008.

Beautiful

Kavanaugh, James. *Will you be my Friend?* Los Angeles, CA: Nash Publishing. 1971.

Sins and Encumbrances

Greene-McCreight, Kathryn. *Darkness Is My Only Companion: A Christian Response to Mental Illness.* Grand Rapids, Michigan: Brazos Press. 2006.

Fear Fight

Poe, Edgar Allan. "Alone." *The Complete Poetry of Edgar Allan Poe (Signet Classics).* New York, New York: Penguin Group (USA). 2008.

Casseroles

Simpson, Amy. *Troubled Minds: Mental Illness and the Church's Mission.* Downers Grove, IL: InterVarsity Press. 2013.

Feeble Faith

Manning, Brennan. *The Ragamuffin Gospel: Good News for the Bedraggled, Beat-Up, and*

Burnt Out. Sisters, Oregon: Multnomah Books. 2005.

Ever After
Downing, Catherine P. Personal Poem.

Resources
Tolstoy, Leo. *Anna Karenina.* Norwalk, Connecticut. The Easton Press. 1975

ABOUT THE AUTHOR

T his book is written under a pseudonym, Catherine, to help protect the privacy of the family. Identifying details are kept to a minimum for the same reason. The author has served as a missionary and now works as an independent communication consultant for faith-based nonprofits. Active in her church as a Bible study leader and intercessor, Catherine also mentors women in issues of faith and faithfulness. She is a contributor to bible.org. A trained teacher for NAMI Family-to-Family classes, Catherine is an advocate for mental health services and legislation. Catherine has been married to Nelson for over 35 years. He continues in mission work, serving alongside some of the least-reached peoples on earth by traveling often from home in the U.S.

CPSIA information can be obtained
at www.ICGtesting.com
Printed in the USA
BVOW06s2112261217
503584BV00022B/255/P